Silk and Silkworms

Wendy Blaxland

Momentum
Silk and Silkworms

First published in Great Britain in 1998 by

Folens Publishers
Albert House
Apex Business Centre
Boscombe Road
Dunstable
Beds LU5 4RL

© 1998 Momentum developed by Barrie Publishing Pty Limited
89 High St, Kew, Vic 3101, Australia
Reprinted 2000

Wendy Blaxland hereby asserts her moral right to be identified as the author of this work in accordance with the Copyright, Designs and Patents Act 1988.
© 1998 Folens Ltd. on behalf of the author.

All rights reserved. No part of this publication may be reproduced or transmitted in any form or by any means, electronic or mechanical, including photocopying, recording or any information storage and retrieval system, without written permission from the publisher.

British Library Cataloguing in Publication Data.
A Catalogue record for this book is available from the British Library

ISBN 1 86202 412 X

Designed by Tom Kurema
Printed in Singapore by PH Productions Pte Ltd

Every effort has been made to contact the owners of the photographs in this book. Where this has not been possible, we invite the owners of the copyright to notify the publishers.

Densey Clyne cover(insert), pp. 1, 5, 6, 7, 8, 9, 11, 12, 14;
Jim Frazier p. 4; Bill Thomas cover, pp. 3, 10.

Have you ever rubbed your cheek against a smooth silk shirt or stroked a soft, fine silk jacket? Have you seen how silk shines? Silk is one of the softest, finest fabrics, often dyed in bright colours.

All of this silk material comes from threads spun from glands found near the mouths of small caterpillars called silkworms.

Farmers in China have kept silkworms for over 3000 years.

When silkworm caterpillars hatch, they are tiny and black.

Silkworms only eat leaves from the mulberry tree.

As they eat and eat, they grow and grow.

5

When silkworms grow too big for their skins, they shed them.

Silkworms shed their skins four times. Each new skin stage is called an instar.

Before they shed their skins, the silkworms stay still or sleep for a day or so. Then they swell up and burst their skins and climb out of them.

While in their last skins, or instars, silkworms eat half of all the food they eat in their lifetime.

You can even hear them eating!

When silkworms are ready to change into moths, they spin cocoons out of silk. The silk comes in one long thread. It takes up to three days for silkworms to spin their cocoons.

After three weeks, the silkworms have changed into moths inside their cocoons.

This photograph shows the approximate size of a fully grown silkworm.

Cocoon opened to show silkworm pupa.

If silkworm farmers want to use the silk from the cocoons, they must kill the silkworms by placing the cocoons into a hot oven. This makes sure the silk stays in one long strand. Otherwise, the moths will break the silk into very short lengths when they eat their way out of the cocoons.

The farmers need at least six strands of silk for one silk thread.

Imagine how many silkworms must spin cocoons to make the silk for one shirt!

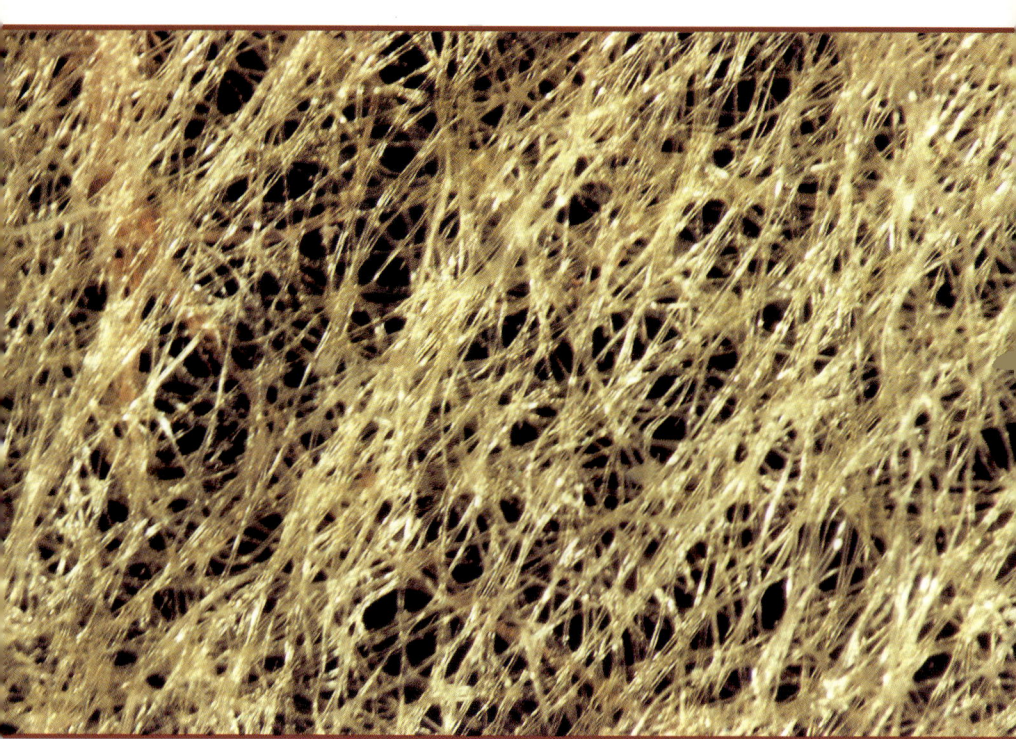

If a moth is allowed to come out of its cocoon, it won't be able to fly. Its wings are useless.

This is because long ago silkworm moths were bred to be flightless so that the farmers could control them.

The small male silkworm moths follow the scent of the bigger female moths. When the males find the females, they mate.

Each female silkworm moth lays up to 500 eggs before she dies.

Next season new silkworms will hatch from these eggs!

Index

caterpillars 3, 4
cheek 3
China 3
cocoon/cocoons 8, 9, 10, 11
eggs 14
fabrics 3
farmers 3, 10, 11
female/females 12, 14
food 6
glands 3
instar/instars 6
jacket 3
leaves 4
male/males 12
material 3
moth/moths 8, 10, 11, 12
mouths 3
mulberry tree 4
oven 10
pupa 9
scent 12
shirt 3, 10
silk 3, 8, 10
silkworm/silkworms 3, 4, 6, 8, 9, 10, 11, 12, 14
skins 6
strand 10
thread/threads 3, 8, 10

Momentum

Titles in Phase 1 Non-fiction Pack D:

A City Garden

Swamps, Marshes and Other Wetlands

Silk and Silkworms

Tropical Rainforests

Giant Pandas

All Kinds of Reptiles

Frogs and Other Amphibians

Being Carried

What's the Difference?

Animal Families

ISBN 1-86202-412-X